CAMBRIAN

THE HORNED MAN

Also by L. M. Boston

The Horned Man

or

Whom will you send to fetch her away?

●

L. M. BOSTON

FABER AND FABER
London

First published in 1970
by Faber and Faber Limited
24 Russell Square London WC1
Printed in Great Britain by
Latimer Trend & Co Ltd Plymouth
All rights reserved

SBN 571 09316 7

Enquiries regarding all performing rights of this play should be addressed to the English Theatre Guild Ltd., Ascot House, 52 Dean Street, London W.1.

DRAMATIS PERSONAE

Sir Martin Westbury

Francis, his son aged eighteen

Philippa, his daughter, aged fifteen

Bess, his daughter aged thirteen

Jenny, his daughter aged ten

Mr. Simon Upjohn, King's Agent

Mistress Alice, governess and housekeeper

Old Mother Alison Taylor

Walter, a page in Sir Martin's house

Cook

Robert Ball, a lout

George Carpenter, a wizened boy

Mat Price, a snivelling boy

Ben Goose, a booby

Tommy Vines, a small talkative hanger-on

Justice Girth, a very fat man

Justice Fever, a neurotic

Justice de Groot, a punisher

A Physician

A Kennel Man

A Secretary

Witch Searcher, Witch Pricker, Mayor, Parson, Crowds

THE SET

The scene is the ante-room to the Tudor hall in Sir Martin's house.

Across the back runs the partition screen with a balustraded gallery from side to side, an exit at each end. Under the gallery is the central door to the hall, the back cloth showing hammer beams. Just left of this door is a staircase at right-angles to the gallery and opening into it. The bottom post of the stairs (left) serves to support the floor of the girls' bedroom, level with the balcony and opening on to it. The bedroom has a lattice left. Underneath the bedroom is the still-room with door front and exit back.

The ante-room has main outside entrance up right, a lattice window down right and an exit to kitchens down left. The fireplace is imagined at the centre front.

Two Tudor chairs, a small table, a bench.

A light-coloured curtain across the door at the back will serve as background to the magistrates' rostrum in the court scene, and also to show the minotaur's shadow in the last scene.

Alice can reach the girls' bedroom either by the stairs on the stage or through to the kitchen and by imagined back stairs to gallery left, where her own room is supposed in the last scene.

Jenny's room is supposed off gallery left.

As this is a close-knit family affair, the running up and down stairs and from one room into another is important.

If the suggested set is too elaborate for an amateur production, rostra can be used instead.

NOTE ON THE MASKS

Alice's mask can be cut off at the point of the upper lip, following the lines of the cheek. The hair to be as long as possible.

Upjohn's mask to cover his shoulders. As the muzzle will rest on his chest, a white gauze blaze on the forehead will serve to see and speak through.

The ghost's mask to be waxen, with a toothless rictus and wild white hair.

The action takes place in the reign of James I.

Act I

The ante-room in Sir Martin's house.
Philippa and Bess looking listlessly out of the window. Jenny on the
stairs nursing her dog.

PHILIPPA
(leaves the window to sit by table)

I am sick of everything. This everlasting flat damp view!
Nothing to look at. No one coming in. No one even going
past. Nothing but mud outside. Nothing but sewing in. When
will anything ever happen! Dominos!
(Dogs barking outside)

BESS

Come back, Philippa. Come and look.

PHILIPPA

What at?

BESS

What are those boys chasing? They are pelting something, or
somebody. Can you see? All huddled up.

PHILIPPA

It's an old woman. Oh! What an old fright. Got her! Got her again, right in the mouth!

BESS

I wish I was a boy. They can do what they like. Open the window. What can I throw? An apple.
(*Philippa opens the lattice and Bess throws. Philippa imitates the old woman's defensive actions. Bess hops in excitement. She throws again.*)

PHILIPPA

She's as easy to hit as an old sheep. Oh! She's fallen backwards into the ditch. The boys are running away. Look out! It will be Father.
(*They close the lattice hastily and stand back giggling.*)
(*Enter Sir Martin right, Walter centre back.*)

PHILIPPA AND BESS
(curtsying)

Good evening, Father.

JENNY

Father! (*She runs towards him but is caught by Philippa and Bess.*)

PHILIPPA

You didn't curtsy. We have to, so must you. Again, properly.
(*Jenny runs and clasps her father.*)

SIR MARTIN

Good evening, my pet. Good evening, girls. Wait a moment, Sweetheart, till I get my wet things off.

WALTER

Your cloak is covered in mud, Sir. Have you had a fall? I hope you have not hurt yourself.

SIR MARTIN

No, thank you, Walter. But just outside here my horse shied and slipped, and I came off. It was so near my own door that I wasn't expecting surprises, but the horse was frightened by an old woman who had fallen in the ditch. I wondered what it was myself, flapping about there, legs in air. Some boys were walking away looking too saintly-smiling to be true, so I guess they had been plaguing the poor old dame. Will you go and find her, Walter, and bring her in to the fire to dry herself and warm up. Tell Cook to give her something to eat.

WALTER

Yes, Sir. (*Exit left.*)

SIR MARTIN

Boys seem little better than a herd of wild dogs. They'll worry anything they can.

BESS

We saw them through the window. I knew that it was very wrong.

SIR MARTIN

I am glad girls have more pity.

JENNY

Father, when you were a little boy, were you cruel?

SIR MARTIN

I am afraid so, once or twice, to try. But I didn't like the feeling, so I stopped. My mother was like you, she couldn't bear it.

JENNY

Where have you been all day?

SIR MARTIN

At the Lord Lieutenant's, discussing very nasty business. I am weary and sick with it, and fear we may be in the middle of it here for a long time. I was glad to be coming home again to you.

PHILIPPA
(*to Bess*)

We're to be in the thick of *something* anyway. That's better than nothing.

JENNY

What is it, Father? May we know?

SIR MARTIN

Ah, my dear, you can't fail to know, and I am afraid you will be as distressed as I am. There is to be an organized witch-hunt, to clear the Fens of witches.

PHILIPPA AND BESS

Witches! Ooooh!

SIR MARTIN

And that means that no helpless old woman will be safe. And even some handsome maids may be singled out, so don't think it has nothing to do with you, Philippa and Bess. It's not justice, it's the Devil's sport.

JENNY

But, Father, are witches real? Can they really make people

die? I thought they were only tales to frighten naughty children with.

Sir Martin

I believe in the Devil. And I suppose it is possible for people to be so wicked that they worship him, and receive from him unnatural powers. It is said that witches have a secret king whom they call The Grand Master, whom they reverence as the Devil's representative. As for their spells, their thorn twigs and finger-nail parings, their boiled blood and newt's eyes, that's all superstitious rubbish, however evil the intention. Though who knows how great the force of an evil intention may be, or where it stops?

The trouble with witch-hunts is that most people have only to be frightened for them to believe that what they fear is true. And if they don't exactly know what it is they fear, they can behave like madmen, and justice means nothing to them. How can you administer justice when all sense of reason has gone? It is not that I disbelieve in the supernatural, but I believe passionately in justice, and in the protection of the innocent. I do not much care if the wicked go free—their evil deeds will catch them up. It matters far more that the innocent shall not be punished. To me, in this "hunt", it will not be the victim alone that I must defend from ignorance and passion. Justice itself will be on trial, and I shall be responsible for keeping it in honour.

But I must not burden you with my troubles. Philippa, my daughter, will you tell Cook that we shall have a visitor from tonight, and that he will be here for supper. And where is Mistress Alice? She should know too. His room must be prepared.

PHILIPPA

A visitor, Father! Who is it? Oh, I suppose it's only the Archdeacon again.

SIR MARTIN

I wish it were. It is the King's Agent come down from London to lead the witch-hunt. As I am one of the Justices I am expected to entertain him. He won't find me helpful to his cause.

PHILIPPA

Have you seen him? What is he like?

BESS

He'll be some old legal fogey. You needn't be so bright-eyed. He's some rheumy old man with bent knees, isn't he, Father? With a drop on the end of his nose. Look at Philippa! She thinks she's going to get married right away.

PHILIPPA

Little beast!

SIR MARTIN

You are silly girls. But you are at the silly age. He is, for a job like this, the worst, the most ruthless type of man there could be—young, ambitious, with his name to make.

PHILIPPA AND BESS

He's young! He's ambitious! (*They start to dance a jig.*) (*Together*) I wonder if he is handsome. (*They link little fingers and wish.*)

SIR MARTIN

Where is Mistress Alice?

PHILIPPA

I expect she's in the still-room as usual. She was making cough syrup ready for the colds we are going to have. And skin-lotion for our hands. Mine are so red.

SIR MARTIN

Go and tell her, Philippa. And Bess, will you please tell Cook. I must take off these muddy clothes. (*Exit up right.*)
(*Jenny goes up into the gallery with her dog Fido. Philippa and Bess cut high-spirited capers.*)

PHILIPPA AND BESS

A visitor! A stranger! A young man! An ambitious young man!

BESS

He may be a hunchback. Or as ugly as a toad.

PHILIPPA

I do hope he'll be handsome. I hope he's handsome and romantic.
(*Enter down left from kitchens, Walter with old Mother Alison Taylor, followed by Cook. Walter puts stool in front of fire and exits, Fido barks.*)

COOK

Sit yourself there, old Mother, and warm yourself up. Why, you're wet through! I saw those boys plaguing you. They've no respect for age.

OLD WOMAN

That's a fine fire! That's good!
(*Philippa and Bess sidle forward arm in arm to stare at the old woman. She gets to her feet to curtsy, knocking over the stool.*)

Old Woman

God bless you, young ladies.
(*They back away and Bess puts her handkerchief to her nose while she speaks.*)

Bess

Father says he is having a very important visitor for supper tonight and you are to prepare a very special meal.

Cook

Very well, young ladies. But I shall need some stores from Mistress Alice. Here you are, Gammer, something to warm your old bones. Sit down to it.

Philippa

I'm going to tell her now. And you'd better get your old grandmother out of the way before the visitor comes, too.

Cook

She can sit there awhile, no one will come yet. She's in no one's way. Look how she trembles. (*She turns her back to set down the pan of soup. As the girls turn to go, Bess hooks away the stool with her foot and the old woman falls, spilling her soup.*) There! Look what you've done. I can't go on heating up soup for you now that I'm busy. (*The girls laugh, and Philippa exit to still-room, Bess goes to sit on the stairs.*)

Cook

There's still some hot in the pan. Take care this time. No good will come to those two young ladies. They are a wild, proud pair.
(*Re-enter Philippa and joins Bess on the stairs.*)

BESS

What a pestilential old thing. She must have been sleeping in farmyards. I say, what if she's a witch? She looks like one. What would happen if she were? Why did you tell Cook to send her away? The visitor might have been pleased. She might be the first catch of the season.

PHILIPPA

I don't want him getting on his hobby-horse the minute he arrives. I want him to have time to notice me.

BESS

Us.

PHILIPPA

You're too young. Me.

BESS

I think I'm quite as pretty as you are. My teeth are smaller. And I can make a dimple. Like this.

PHILIPPA

Then you wouldn't be able to talk. Or kiss.

BESS

Oh mercy! Kiss whom?

PHILIPPA

Who knows?

BESS

The Parson! (*Laughter.*)

PHILIPPA

The Parson! (*Hysterics of laughter.*)

Bess

I say, there's Father's little sweetheart, his little innocent. How about telling her there's a witch in front of the fire?
(*They suck in their lips over their teeth and make clawing sighs, and nod to each other.*)

Philippa

Sweetheart!

Bess

Mousie, mousie, mousie, mousie!

Jenny

What is it? (*They crouch by her, whispering.*)

Philippa

Sh! Something very frightening has happened. I'm shaking with fear. We must warn you about it, because you are such a trustful innocent.

Bess

Sh! Be careful, Philippa, *she* might hear.

Philippa

Oh, do you think. . . . Jenny, down there, she's a witch. She has no teeth and hands like claws.

Bess

She looks like the Devil himself, crouching there all in black. I thought I saw him peep out from under her skirts. That's why I tipped up her stool, to see if he would run out.

Philippa

He went up the chimney. Devils are used to fire.

JENNY

(*after a moment of alarm, laughs*)

You're making it up to frighten me. It's only the old woman
you were throwing things at. (*Enter Walter down right,
pauses.*)

BESS

Because she's a witch. We wanted her to go away, not to
come here. But Father would bring her in.

PHILIPPA

Even after what she did to him.

JENNY

What did she do to him?

BESS

She made the Sign of the Cross with her bare legs in the air.
That's *very* wicked. Only witches do that.

PHILIPPA

To make his horse shy and throw him. He might have broken
his neck. (*Exit Walter centre back.*)

JENNY

Oh no!

PHILIPPA

Just come and peep at her. You'll see. She's a horribly old
thing, with the Evil Eye. (*They drag Jenny downstairs and push
her forward. The old woman is dozing and warming her bare
shins.*)

JENNY

Good evening, old mother. Are you warmer now?

OLD WOMAN

God bless you, little love. Sitting here I'm as warm as a queen. Keep your dog away, little lady. I've neither shoes nor hose if he should bite.

PHILIPPA

(*pulling Jenny away*)

Come away, you little fool. She's put the Evil Eye on your precious Fido.

JENNY

She hasn't!

BESS

She did. I saw it. And she pointed too. After all, Fido did bark when she came in. Good dog, Fido, good dog! He knew.

PHILIPPA

Good dog! (*They both scamper upstairs laughing and exit via gallery Left. After a long pause Jenny comes forward again.*)

JENNY

Old mother, I know it's nice and warm here, but go away. (*Enter Cook.*) Please go away quickly, now.

COOK

Why, my dear, what's the matter? That behaviour is not like you. It's unkind.

JENNY

I'm frightened.

COOK

What of, lovey? You've nothing to be frightened of.

JENNY

But I am. For her. And for Father too.

COOK

For your Father! What have you got in your little head!

JENNY

Tell her to go, Cook. My sisters may make mischief.

OLD WOMAN

(*resignedly*)

I'll go, little lady. Thank you, ma'am for the soup. It's a lovely fire to leave. (*Exit left.*)

COOK

Mischief's quickly done as I know. And a great satisfaction to those that do it. I don't suppose she has anywhere to go, either.

JENNY

What will she do?

COOK

I don't know, I'm sure, poor thing.

JENNY

I'm sorry. (*She goes to window and presses herself in the window-seat.*)
(*Enter Alice, from still-room. She is young, big, handsome, with a face like a pale mask. She is remote and makes no pretension to be part of the family. As housekeeper she goes in and out of the rooms at will, walking superbly and checking to listen or glance now and then. She laughs briefly, but never smiles, except once. She now*

23

stands, centre, with a large bunch of keys, and moves her head, questing like an animal. Her voice is low, sexy but offhand.)

ALICE

I sense a stirring of evil.

CURTAIN

SCENE II

The girls' bedroom. Alice dressing Philippa's hair. Bess looking on.

PHILIPPA

Just fancy—a young gentleman from London! We never see anything but old men. Just because Mother died, Father needn't make us all live like hermits. It's two years now, and we've hardly met a young man since last year's skating. I thought when my brother Francis went to Cambridge he would bring his friends for hunting or coursing. You would think so. But with Father so sober and gloomy I suppose it is more fun anywhere else. We have to stay mewed up here, in old-fashioned clothes and not knowing the new way to talk. You sound like a fool if you don't know it.

ALICE

Frowning spoils your face, Philippa. And it is never wise to show your feelings. You have a great advantage over other people if they have no idea what you think. You must learn to *wear* your face—not just to have it. You could practise even here. For instance, it would be difficult to fox Bess. You could have fun that way. It would be quite an art. Your Father would be easy enough, but your manner to him so far would deceive nobody. Roll your eyes up, Philippa. I'll put some drops in to brighten them.

PHILIPPA

OW!

ALICE

There. Look up at me now. Oh. Swimming with tears and very fetching. It takes a moment or two to stop smarting.

PHILIPPA

I have put on my new point lace collar. Is it right?

ALICE

First you can sit here with your hands in this bowl. They need softening. Your turn, Bess.

PHILIPPA

Isn't she too young to be dressed up?

ALICE

She's old enough to be married.

PHILIPPA

She!!

ALICE

Scowling again. You are a bad pupil. She is very pretty. (*Philippa smirks.*) That's better. I see you are learning.

BESS

Am I prettier than she is?

ALICE

(She watches Philippa who changes to an arrogant who-cares smile. Alice laughs)

What a question. Every pretty girl, if she is clever, surrounds herself with other pretty girls, so that the young man she wants will enjoy himself among so many, and still see that she is the most attractive.

PHILIPPA AND BESS

(Looking at each other)

Oh.

ALICE

It needs self-control, and no scowling. Change places with Philippa, Bess. Now, Philippa, let me see to that collar. Good. Lastly, some of my muskrose perfume on your neck and bosom. There. And some for Bess.

PHILIPPA

Oh, no!

ALICE

Now, now!

PHILIPPA

But we can't both smell exactly alike. That would be too ridiculous.

ALICE

It would rather. Bess can have violet oil.

BESS

Ooh! Don't I smell lovely!

ALICE

Now you are both ready. I can't do any more. See what you can do.

PHILIPPA

Do you think he will talk to us? What shall we say to him?

ALICE

Something he might like to hear. If you can think of anything. It sounds as if he has arrived. We will go down. All set?

The scene changes to the ante-room.

(Movements of servants, sounds of horses and arrivals. Sir Martin comes into the ante-room from centre back, holding Jenny by the hand. Alice, Philippa and Bess come down stairs and stand left.)

WALTER

Mr. Simon Upjohn.

(Enter Mr. Upjohn, right. He is a brutally handsome teenage idol, ultra fashionable in black with bold eyes and very flexible manners. He wears a red ribbon garter on his right leg and a black on his left. Colours reversed on wrists. Walter takes his cloak and hat.)

SIR MARTIN

Welcome to our house, Mr. Upjohn. We cannot entertain you in the London style, but please make the best of our country comforts.

UPJOHN

I am greatly honoured.

SIR MARTIN

I hope your journey was good?

UPJOHN

Do not take it personally if I say the roads in your county are abominably muddy and pot-holed, and even under water for a long stretch. But we met with no robbers on the way and I did not need my sword. (*Unbuckles it and hands it to Walter. Exit Walter.*)

SIR MARTIN

We don't anticipate robbers here. We are too far from the London road. Now, Mr. Upjohn, this is my youngest daughter Jenny. (*She curtsies.*)

UPJOHN

A pretty child. (*He tries to chuck her under the chin, but she backs away to her father.*)
And clearly, from the way she clings to you, your favourite.

SIR MARTIN

I am sorry if I let it be seen so clearly. She resembles her dear mother, whom I have lost.

UPJOHN
(*bowing*)

My condolences.

SIR MARTIN

My son is not here. He is studying law in Cambridge. My eldest daughter, Philippa.
(*Upjohn bows, she curtsies and then naïvely holds out her hand. He kisses it, she wriggles.*)

UPJOHN

Court manners for a young lady who would grace St. James's.

PHILIPPA
(*genteelly*)

Are you much at Court, Sir?

Do not make fun of me, charming Mistress Philippa. I am in the courts every day, pursuing his August Majesty the Devil, which is my calling. For this reason, I often have cause to wait upon His Majesty King James, who takes a keen interest. In his ante-chamber one may wait for hours, but the time is pleasantly spent as persons of the highest rank are waiting too. There is a great exchange of compliment and interest.

PHILIPPA

Fancy that, Bess!

SIR MARTIN

My younger daughter, Bess.

UPJOHN

So this is Bess. She is perhaps not yet too old to be saluted on the cheek. (*Kisses her.*) A visiting friend is always some-what in the position of an uncle.
(*The two girls glare at each other, with grins, and Bess makes her dimple.*)

Had I known that I was coming into so charming a family of young girls, I would have tried to bring each a little gift from London. As it is, I have only brought His Majesty's learned book on Witchcraft, which I would like to offer you, Sir, if you don't already possess it.

SIR MARTIN

You are most kind. This lady is my housekeeper, Mistress Alice.
(*They salute each other off-handedly.*)

Come, Mr. Upjohn, sit down. Let me offer you a tankard of mulled ale until supper is ready. Walter! Bring some mulled ale. (*To Jenny*.) My pet, go and sit with your sisters.

UPJOHN

I must apologize for the length of time I may have to trouble your hospitality. I will do my best to get His Majesty's business done as quickly as possible.

SIR MARTIN

It is an honour to entertain the King's emissary. And justice cannot be hurried.
(*Enter Walter with tankards.*)

WALTER

May I offer some to Mr. Upjohn's Secretary who is in the servants' hall?

SIR MARTIN

Of course, of course. I do not think you will find much devilry in or around our quiet country town. It is a prosperous law-abiding district. Neighbourly folk.

UPJOHN

I am afraid you may be rudely awakened. Human nature is the same all the world over, and my little investigation will be like a miniature Day of Judgement. There is nothing hid that shall not be made known and the secrets of all hearts shall be revealed.

SIR MARTIN

There have been no accusations, nor have I heard any rumours of witchcraft for years.

UPJOHN

The accusations will come. The very fact that there is an

investigation of witchcraft here proves that there are witches to be examined.

SIR MARTIN

No, Sir. It does not.

UPJOHN

(*laughing*)

Of course it does not. But people will think it does. Everyone who has ever injured anyone—and your innocent country folk are not above a dirty trick now and again—will remember some unexplained accident to themselves that *could* have been revenge, and the sick will think of someone who could be sitting watching a candle burn down and willing them to die as it goes out. And as the snowball grows, everyone will begin to remember the Devil whom all fear in their hearts more than God. And then every tongue will be loosed. Oh, there will be accusations enough.
(*Enter Walter with a note.*)

WALTER

Your Secretary asked that I would deliver this to you, Sir.

UPJOHN

(*continuing*)

Accusations enough. And everyone will believe them. Excuse me, Sir Martin. (*Opens, reads, writes a few words.*) Ask him to see to that right away.
(*Exit Walter.*)

SIR MARTIN

I should be very grieved to see trouble and back-biting among my neighbours, or among those who serve me.

Yes, I am sure. And there's the family circle to think of too. Very disturbing. It is usually their relatives that people hate or fear most. You, of course, cannot fear that. What a charming group they make! But the devil nudges in where he can.

I wonder, Mr. Upjohn, if your method of working does not aid him more than it hinders, and leave the world worse than it was.

Unfortunately, my fish is only caught in troubled waters. You must admit that it is a man's first business to do thoroughly what he has undertaken. To do myself justice, I get results. And from what I see in the course of my investigation, the world could hardly be worse than it is.
(*Enter Walter, centre back.*)

Supper is served, Sir. (*Exit.*)

Come, Mr. Upjohn. Shall I lead the way?
(*Upjohn steps back and motions to Philippa to go first. He bows as she goes past. She is embarrassed and drops half a curtsy. Bess follows with saucy looks. Jenny gets a sweeping ironic bow and runs past. Alice and Upjohn stand face to face for a deep look. She throws her head back and smiles. He makes in the air the sign of the Cross backward [right–left, down–up] quickly, as if he were shaking back the lace of his cuff. She gives a long reverential curtsy and kisses his red garter.*)

ALICE

Grand Master! My lord!
(*She precedes him to exit.*)

CURTAIN

SCENE III

The ante-room. Next morning.
*Philippa and Bess on the gallery, arms on each other's shoulders,
looking down.*

PHILIPPA

I wonder if he's up yet. I would think he would get up early.
He's so vital.

BESS

Wasn't it a change last night from watching Father and the
Vicar playing chess. Mr. Upjohn laughs so well—you have
to laugh with him.

PHILIPPA

He laughed enough at you playing your little piece on the
lute.

BESS

That was because I was pulling faces at him.

PHILIPPA

It was fun singing madrigals. A tenor voice comes creeping
up my spine somehow. He kept looking at me in 'Love do
not deny me'.

BESS

That was to try to keep you on the right note.

PHILIPPA

Pig! You are jealous.

BESS

Nothing to be jealous of.

PHILIPPA

That's all you know!

BESS

What, then?

PHILIPPA

Well, I told him about the old woman yesterday. I thought he would like to know. He said some very complimentary things to me afterwards.

BESS

You do think you are Somebody. I told him too.

PHILIPPA

You did! When?

BESS

When we were looking through the sheets of music. Looking for 'Love do not deny me', no doubt.

PHILIPPA

What did he say to you?

BESS

Wouldn't you like to know! Sh! (*They take up elegant attitudes over the stair rail. Enter below Sir Martin and Mr. Upjohn,*

34

back. At the same time Walter admits the Secretary at entrance right.)

UPJOHN

I was sorry to hear, Sir, that your horse threw you yesterday. I hope you were feeling no ill effects while you were entertaining me. Is there much stiffness this morning? (*To Secretary.*) Good day.

SIR MARTIN

Good day, Mr. Secretary. (*They walk on.*) Who told you about my fall? It was not worth mentioning. My horse shied and his hind feet slipped in the mud. I simply rolled off on to soft ground. It was nothing.

UPJOHN

I am glad to hear it. You were fortunate. What caused your horse to shy, at the end of a long journey, at his own gate?

SIR MARTIN

The unexpected sight of an old woman lying in the ditch, poor old thing.

UPJOHN

I am glad to have your own voluntary statement. Make a note of that, Mr. Secretary.

SIR MARTIN

What sort of procedure is this? I am making no statement to you. I am in my own house talking, as I thought, to a guest. Explain yourself and the presence of your unwanted Secretary.

UPJOHN

Forgive my little stratagem. If we were in a court of law I could hardly question the justice. But a voluntary statement

35

from you could have a good effect. After all, what have you said? That your horse shied at an old woman in a ditch. The barest statement that could be made, and of unquestionable truth. The *barest* statement! Quite amusing. I am told her bare legs were waving in the air.

SECRETARY

Ha ha!

UPJOHN

You are not in a court of law now. Kindly behave with proper respect.

SIR MARTIN
(*to Secretary*)

Get out of here at once. (*Exit Secretary.*)
It is an outrage.

UPJOHN

As for the second part of your protest, my dear host, that I was not behaving like a guest—if an accusation is made by a member of your own household, I assume you would prefer the preliminary sifting to be done with as much privacy as possible?

SIR MARTIN

What you suggest is hideous. I cannot accept it.

UPJOHN

I told you the accusations would come.
(*The girls shrink out of sight.*)

SIR MARTIN
(*sitting down heavily*)

Who in my household has accused whom?

UPJOHN

Come now, come now! Such a weight of discouragement will put ideas into my head! Our business only concerns a wandering stranger—a mere beggar.

SIR MARTIN

If anyone in my household has borne false witness against a stranger or anyone else, rich or poor, I will see to it that they suffer the full rigour of the law. There is a penalty for false witness. There is nothing angers me so absolutely as trumped-up charges.

UPJOHN

It becomes you. You look like Jove himself. But swearing to a reasonable suspicion is not perjury, even if it prove unfounded. As it rarely does, witchcraft being so widespread.

SIR MARTIN

God have mercy on us all! Idle chatter from the servants, I suppose. I thought better of them all.

UPJOHN

Idle chatter is the natural relief of servants. And its best spice is repetition of what is said *in here*.

SIR MARTIN

What! What are you hinting?

UPJOHN

You yourself sent the old woman in here. Shall we call in Walter?

SIR MARTIN

Walter? He's not been here long. Still hardly more than a

boy. But a good one, or so I thought. I will hear what Walter has to say, but I will question him myself.

UPJOHN

Certainly. Certainly.

SIR MARTIN

Walter!

(*Enter Walter.*)

Come here, boy. Now, Walter, you have not been with me long, but I know your parents well and I think well of you. I believe you tell the truth, and you must tell it now.

WALTER

Yes, Sir.

SIR MARTIN

What is this story you have been repeating in the kitchen, accusing that poor old woman of witchcraft—about whom none of us know anything, either good or bad, except that she seems destitute?

WALTER

I didn't accuse anybody, honestly, Sir. I only repeated in the servants' hall what Mistress Philippa and her sister said. We always repeat what the young ladies say. It makes for laughter and conversation. And it was funny, what she said.

SIR MARTIN

Go on, boy. What did she say?

WALTER

Mistress Philippa said the old woman was a witch and had

38

made your horse throw you on purpose, and you might have
been killed.

SIR MARTIN

That was found laughable in the kitchen?

WALTER

No, Sir. But Mistress Bess said the witch lay on her back and
made the sign of the Cross with her bare legs in the air. I . . . I
thought that was funny, Sir.

UPJOHN

It's always unwise to laugh at the Devil, boy.

WALTER

It wouldn't have been funny if it was true, Sir, but it was
little Mistress Bess saying a thing like that.

SIR MARTIN

Bess too! You were not there, Walter, when my horse shied.
You met me only after I had given my horse to the groom.
The old woman had fallen on her back, head downwards in
the ditch, pushed, I am afraid, by some boys. Robert Bell
and his lot. If her legs were in the air that was because she
couldn't help it and was trying to right herself. Do you
understand that?

WALTER

Yes, Sir.

SIR MARTIN

I see. I am sure you never meant the harm you have done,
but to prevent worse, I charge you never to alter the simple
truth of your story. It puts the blame, I know, on my

daughters, who were guilty of almost unforgivable folly, but not on the old woman who was guilty of nothing.

WALTER

Yes, Sir.

SIR MARTIN

Now go and call my two elder daughters.
(*Walter goes up to bedroom door.*)

WALTER

Mistress Philippa, Mistress Bess!

PHILIPPA AND BESS

What is it, Walter?

WALTER

Your father wants to speak to you both.

BESS

Does he look angry?

WALTER

Very stern, Mistress Bess.

PHILIPPA

Oh, dear! Now for it. Come on, then, Bess. We are too old to be beaten. At least I am. After all, we only said what we thought.
(*They go down, reluctantly and curtsy to both men. Exit Walter.*)

SIR MARTIN

Come here, my daughters. I am very greatly displeased with what I hear about your wanton, unfounded talk yesterday

40

afternoon. You are reported to have said that a harmless old woman was a witch. Did you make such an accusation?

(*The girls look in consternation at Upjohn, who smiles deprecatingly.*)

UPJOHN

Young ladies, please forgive my presence at a moment of parental displeasure, which would normally be private. In my capacity as Prosecutor I must be present when this little matter is cleared up.

SIR MARTIN

What have you to say for yourselves?
(*Silence.*)
Do you admit having said such a thing?

PHILIPPA

————Yes, Father.

BESS

Yes, Father.

UPJOHN

I see you have two truthful girls, who would not alter their story to suit the hearer.

SIR MARTIN

To whom did you tell this monstrous story?

BOTH

To Jenny.

SIR MARTIN

Why? Why did you say this cruel thing to a trusting child?

PHILIPPA

To warn her, because she is so trusting.

SIR MARTIN

Were you not teasing her, as you often do?

BOTH

Oh no, Father.

SIR MARTIN

You were making stories up for play?

PHILIPPA

No, Father.

SIR MARTIN

But you had absolutely no reason for thinking the old woman was a witch. Don't tell me about her poor old legs.

PHILIPPA

I saw her shake her fist at the house. And then afterwards she made your horse throw you.

(*Upjohn nods approval. Enter Alice on gallery left; seen only by Upjohn.*)

BESS

And then Jenny's precious Fido barked at the old woman, and she pointed at him and cast the Evil Eye on him, and Jenny went away crying.

(*Bess looks at Upjohn for approval, but only gets an ironic look.*)

SIR MARTIN

And has anything happened to Fido?

No, not yet.

(*Alice nods. Exit Alice.*)

SIR MARTIN

Not yet! Oh in the name of God, you weary me with your malicious, ignorant nonsense. What can one do in such a quicksand of irresponsible folly? You have started the Devil's work. Do you understand that this old creature will have to suffer all the ordeals—which prove nothing either way, but may result in her being hanged though innocent? Go to your room and stay there till you come to your senses. You disgrace me. Don't think I shall temper the law for you. It is not too late to confess that you were inventing stories for some idiotic satisfaction of your own. You are not under oath yet. But you will be. Go.

(*Exeunt Philippa and Bess upstairs. Sir Martin paces about in a fury while Upjohn sits swinging his gartered leg.*)

This is adolescent hysteria. At their age girls are the most irrational, irritating creatures. You really would think sometimes the Devil was in them. But it means nothing—nothing. I beg you, Sir, for God's sake, not for mine, dismiss this as the nonsense it is.

UPJOHN

I regret, Sir Martin. It has gone too far already. When my Secretary sent me word last night, I started enquiries. The old woman is already in custody. The case must be brought. I have no doubt that with you, Sir, on the Bench, she will have a fair trial. But even should she be acquitted, she will have startled the neighbourhood into a more profitable state of terror. We need a climate of suspicion.

43

SIR MARTIN

Allow me to tell you, Sir, that you are an exceedingly wicked man.

UPJOHN

(*jovially*)

No offence taken. Personal opinions are allowed. You, Sir, were trying to influence witnesses.

SIR MARTIN

They are my daughters, even if I am a Justice.

UPJOHN

I'm not objecting. I don't object, because if they are afraid of you—as they obviously are—such an awe-inspiring display of wrath as you have just given will only make them cling to their story. By so doing at least they save their importance. If they retract, they are reduced to naughty children. Their best hope is for me to win the case.

Dare I say, so early in the game, Check!

CURTAIN

SCENE IV

The girls' bedroom and the ante-room.

BESS

Oh dear! We have got ourselves into trouble now. I've never seen Father in such a rage.

PHILIPPA

He didn't say much, but he was in a rage all right. I don't

see why that smelly old ragbag matters so much—more than his own daughters. You can see he's not going to do anything to save our faces. How could we say we had made it all up when we had both said it to Mr. Upjohn? I only said it to make conversation. Alice told us to say anything that would interest him.

Bess

It's a good thing we have Mr. Upjohn on our side.

Philippa

Do you think that? It is true he didn't give us away. I mean, he didn't say we had told him.

Bess

It's more than that. He needs us. We are in it together.

Philippa

You are bright for your age, Bess. (*Dreamily.*) We could help his career.

Bess

He will be very splendid in court. All the girls will be watching him, and see us there talking to him. He'll have to be rather special with us, because we don't have to do it. If we went back on it he would look a fool.

Philippa

He'll never do that. But he is bound to be grateful to us. Nothing Father can threaten will make me go back on it now.

Bess

You'll be a martyr for love, I suppose.

PHILIPPA

All the same, it will be frightening with Father sitting there in glory. What if Father is cleverer than he is?

BESS

Father isn't clever. He's only old and respected.

PHILIPPA

Father's sent for Francis to come from Cambridge and defend her. They will make quite a strong side, both being local too. It will be two against one. And Francis is very good-looking.

BESS

Two against three.

PHILIPPA

Don't exaggerate your own importance, you silly. Why ever did you say that about the old creature putting the Evil Eye on Fido? You only did it to get into the conversation.

BESS

You call it conversation, with Father in a rage like that? I had to say something.

PHILIPPA

But Fido is perfectly well. After all, the horse shied before we said so.

(*They start giggling and then laugh wildly.*)

BESS

(*imitating her father*)

"A quicksand of irresponsible folly." Poor Father. He really minds.

(*Enter Alice.*)

ALICE

You sound quite merry.

PHILIPPA AND BESS TOGETHER

What have you brought? Oh, dry bread and milk again.

BESS

Nothing else?

ALICE

Nothing else.

BESS

What are you having downstairs?

ALICE

Trout. Roast wild boar and glazed apples.

BOTH

Oooh!

ALICE

Pigeon pie, sherry syllabub.

BOTH

Oooh!

ALICE

Peaches in brandy.

BESS

Oh, it's too bad. Will Francis be there?

ALICE

He will be.

47

BESS

How long have we got to stay here?

ALICE

Till repentance or till after the trial—except for your appearance at it, of course.

PHILIPPA

Is it like a funeral, or do we wear our best clothes?

ALICE

It is more like a party. Everyone who is "appearing"—except the prisoner of course—makes the best impression they can.

PHILIPPA

Hooray! Not that our best is very good. Could I be making new rosettes for my shoes? Look at them, they are crushed. Can I have some ribbon?

BESS

How's Fido?

ALICE

Fido? He's very frisky. Why do you ask?

BESS

I'm not nervous about the trial, not really, except about this Fido business. He's too well.

ALICE

You should have thought of that before.

BESS

How long does the Evil Eye take to work?

48

Days. Weeks. Months. But in this case unless it works before the trial tomorrow it will be no help to you. The first part of your story is feeble enough, and the second part feebler. I'll get you the ribbon, Philippa. Your brother may make you look a fool at the trial, but at least you can show a pretty foot.

(*Exit Alice, via gallery.*)

PHILIPPA

Francis! Why does this have to be such a family affair? He knows too much about us. A brother isn't fair.
(*They sit sulking with their elbows on the table.*)

PHILIPPA

(*screams*)

Dominos! (*She thumps them with her fist, hurts herself and cries.*)

BESS

I've got an idea.

PHILIPPA

What?

BESS

It's rather naughty.

PHILIPPA

Naughty! How old do you think you are?

BESS

I do have that sort of feeling about it.　　But it can't be helped now. It won't do any real harm.

(*Re-enter Alice, via gallery left.*)

ALICE

Here are your ribbons, Philippa. That will keep you busy for a while. I'll take the tray down now.

BESS

I haven't finished my milk. Don't rush away. We're tired of being alone. I want to talk to you.

ALICE

I'm busy downstairs. I can't stay.

BESS

Well, bring Fido up then. He's better than nothing. I am so bored.

(*Alice makes as if to go.*)

Wait, wait. And I need some of your physic. I think I need a good strong dose.

ALICE

Do you think so? Very well. I'll bring Fido and the physic. (*Goes downstairs and exits by still-room.*)

PHILIPPA

So that's what you are going to do.

BESS

It won't hurt him. We take it ourselves. But his symptoms will certainly be noticed. Imagine the interrupted supper party! Quick, quick!! (*They laugh.*)
It's a good thing we can laugh.

PHILIPPA

I hear horses. It must be Francis arriving. (*They rush to the window right.*)

Yes, there he is.

BESS

And Father.

PHILIPPA

And Mr. Upjohn!!

BESS

Doesn't Father look shabby beside them? Francis is really stylish in a quiet sort of way.

PHILIPPA

But not like Mr. Upjohn.

BESS

Oh no. Not like him!

PHILIPPA

I wish we were downstairs. Shut up here and made to look like children in his eyes. I can't bear it.

(*Re-enter Alice. She runs upstairs with Fido under her arm.*)

ALICE

Here's Fido. And your physic, Bess. I brought two in case Philippa wanted one as well. Take it in milk. I must run. Francis is here. I'll be back later.

BESS

Don't be long.

(*Alice starts down the stairs.*)

BESS

Come on, Fido. Come to be made a fuss of. You've got to have some physic, do you know?

PHILIPPA

One's enough. We might have to give him some more tomorrow. I'll put the other in this box, see? Here. We'll say we each had one.

BESS

Bring the milk. Now then, Fido, be a good dog. (*They dose him.*) There. Good dog. All gone. Wipe his whiskers, Philippa, he's all milky. Poor Fido. You've had physic before. It's only gripes.

(*Sits with Fido on her lap. Party sounds downstairs. Enter Walter from centre back, Sir Martin, Upjohn, Francis, Jenny from entrance right.*)

SIR MARTIN

It is good to have you here, my dear boy. You have wasted no time. I am most unhappy about this affair.

FRANCIS

I know you are, Father. I am afraid Mr. Upjohn must think you have called in a very inexperienced opponent for him.

SIR MARTIN

You must not underrate him, Mr. Upjohn. Though he is young, he brings from Cambridge a brilliant reputation.

UPJOHN

We will cross swords with all the more pleasure when the time comes.

FRANCIS

(to Jenny)

Well, my sweet little ha'porth, why do I only get half a welcome? Where's the other half of the penny, Fido? I expect a whirl of welcome from him.

JENNY

I thought he was here. Where *is* Fido? Fido!

ALICE

(curtsying to Francis)

I'll get him, Jenny. I saw him in the kitchen just now.
(Exit left.)

SIR MARTIN

Come on through into the hall, all of you. Come, Jenny.
(Exeunt centre back.)
(Girls' bedroom. Enter Alice from gallery Left.)

ALICE

Finished with the physic and Fido? Jenny's calling for him. I'll take him.
(Exit left.)

BESS

Did she know?

CURTAIN

SCENE V

The ante-room. Next morning.

53

Sir Martin, Francis, Kennelman, Alice and Jenny bending over Fido.

KENNELMAN

That warn't no distemper, Sir. 'Twas poison. Couldn't be anything else with those symptoms.

SIR MARTIN

Where would he get it? He's always fed in the house. Jenny sees to him herself.

JENNY

Is he dead, Alice?

ALICE

Yes. Oh yes. He's dead. (*Holds him up by back legs like a rabbit.*)

JENNY

Poor F—F—F (*Bursts into tears and runs to her father.*)

KENNELMAN

Poor little maid!

FRANCIS

Could the old woman have done it?

SIR MARTIN

In God's name, I hope not. Jenny, my darling, control your-self. Look up, there, there. Tell me, sweetheart, did the old woman give him anything to eat?

JENNY

Nooooo.

KENNELMAN

It will be the Evil Eye, like Miss Bess said.

SIR MARTIN

So everyone will say. But saying nonsense doesn't make it true. Have you been buying ratbane from any of those pedlars?

KENNELMAN

No, Sir. It's too dangerous.

SIR MARTIN

Come, my love. You shall have another Fido just like him, and you'll love him just as much.

(*Jenny continues crying.*)

Mistress Alice, the kennelman will take him away. Do you go please and see that those shameless girls are ready in time.

(*Exeunt Alice and Kennelman.*)

FRANCIS

This will make my defence much more difficult. You see the kennelman is half convinced already.

SIR MARTIN

The people you have to convince are the other three justices. They can outvote me.

FRANCIS

What are they likely to think?

SIR MARTIN

Girth will agree with everybody all the way through. If the crowd shout to save her he will join them. But I greatly fear they will shout for her execution. She is a stranger, you see. If you could persuade Girth, we should be even numbers and the trial would at least be postponed. Of the other two,

Fever is a superstitious fellow. He fears everything and the Evil Eye most. De Groot believes that a Justice is there to condemn everyone regardless. The Prosecutor will do what he likes with those two, but the crowd has some influence.

FRANCIS

You seem to have brought me here in the certainty that I must fail.

SIR MARTIN

You will find that is the normal situation of anyone talking simple sense when passions have been worked up. If you can keep a breath of cool common sense alive in the Court and even a little decency, we might possibly get her acquitted. It won't be easy. You may even begin to wonder whether to be sane and just is not the only real madness. But at least this time I shall know there are two of us.

FRANCIS

Thank you, Father.

SIR MARTIN

And you, Jenny, you're one of us. Come, wipe your eyes. Let's go and see Francis's new horse. Bring an apple for him.

(*Exeunt right.*)

(*Enter Upjohn centre back, and Alice descending the stairs. She curtsies.*)

UPJOHN

This was your doing?

ALICE

No, my lord. I work with more subtlety than that. I let the young ladies think of it themselves and do it themselves.

And more will come of it, for they will know now how to use it and will see how useful it is.

UPJOHN

Are you planning that they shall be the next accused? What would their most honourable father do then?

ALICE

Hang them, I should think. They are quite out of favour. His precious Jenny would be a better target, but even you, my Lord, would never make anyone believe it of her. Forgive me for doubting your powers. But the girls are well away. That dim-wit Philippa will gaze at you in Court like a dog drooling at the food on its master's plate. Sh!

(*She starts and runs halfway up stairs. Exit Upjohn centre.*)

CURTAIN

SCENE VI

The girls' bedroom.
Philippa and Bess within.

PHILIPPA

Yesterday I was so excited about today. Something going on for once, all the neighbours coming. I thought it would be like a play.

BESS

With Mr. Upjohn as the leading man and you as the leading lady.

PHILIPPA

Well, he will be there, that's certain. But I feel so worked up and shaky. Don't you?

BESS

Yes. I feel frightened. I don't know why. (*Enter Alice.*)
Oh, at last! What was all the commotion about downstairs?

ALICE

Jenny was crying about Fido.

BESS

Isn't he well today?

ALICE

He's dead. The kennelman said he was poisoned.
(*Shocked silence.*)

BESS

But I thought————we thought——

ALICE

You both thought the old witch had put the Evil Eye on him.
(*Silence.*)
Well, she must have done, mustn't she? So really you don't have to worry about the trial any more. The case is proved. Now, come along. Get ready.

BESS

What will they do to the old woman?

ALICE

Everything they can think of.

BESS

Oh, Father will stop them.

ALICE

He won't be able to. How are your shoes, Philippa? Show me.

PHILIPPA
(*posturing*)

Do I stand like this? Or like this?
(*While they are busy, Bess looks quickly in the box.*)

BESS
(*aside*)

It's gone! Which of them has it? It's dangerous.

ALICE

What's the matter, Bess? Aren't you feeling well? You haven't got gripes, have you, after that physic? (*Shakes her.*) Have you?

BESS

I'm all right now. Where's my kerchief?

PHILIPPA
(*still posturing*)

My shoes look really quite taking. I am going to enjoy myself after all. Being asked questions by him and always giving him the answer he wants seems somehow rather like a love scene.

CURTAIN

Act II

SCENE I

The Court Room in Sir Martin's house. The Justices's rostrum centre back. Below, Clerk, Prosecutor and Counsel.
Witnesses (Philippa, Bess, Jenny, 5 boys), right.
Parson, Physician, Mayor, left.
Dock down left. Crowds on gallery and stairs.
Witch Searcher, Witch Pricker, Constables and Alison Taylor wait extreme left.
All stand as Justices enter.

JUSTICE FEVER
(*to Girth*)

They say at night the witches dance with the Devil himself and that he roars like a bull. There's no decent word for the goings on.

GIRTH

Well, your dancing days are over anyway. And mine!

DE GROOT

We'll burn them out, root and branch. It's the only way.
(*Justices take their seats.*)

SIR MARTIN

Bring in the accused.

(*Alison Taylor, obviously the worse for rough treatment, is led forward by Witch Searcher and Witch Pricker.*)

CLERK

Alison Taylor, you stand accused of witchcraft in that on the afternoon of January 12th you did by making an obscene sign cause the horse of Sir Martin Westbury to throw him, whereby he might have been killed, and that afterwards in his house you did cast the Evil Eye upon his daughter's dog and caused it to die. How say you, are you guilty or not guilty.

OLD WOMAN

I done nothing.

SIR MARTIN

Alison Taylor, have you anything you wish to say?

OLD WOMAN

Yes, Sir, thank you kindly, Sir. It was good by your fire. It was as good a fire as I've seen this many a year.

SIR MARTIN

You see, gentlemen, that she is of a great simplicity. Alison Taylor, whether you have done anything or not, it is much easier to prove guilt even when it does not exist, than to prove innocence. But I will see that you have fair trial and all the protection that the law allows. Gentlemen, the prisoner has been searched by the Witch Searcher in the presence of the Parson, the Physician and his wife, and the Witch Pricker, and no Devil's marks were found on her.

Fever

Was she searched thoroughly in every part?

Physician

Yes, Your Worship, and to my mind with grievous rough-
ness.

Fever

If they had been thorough they would have found something,
that I know.

Upjohn

My case against the accused is that she, being a person from a
distance, without occupation or address, and having no good
business in this place, was making her way towards Sir
Martin's house at the time (which she could have known)
when he was due to return. Some of the sons of his tenants
were trying to drive her off—you may think out of loyalty—
when she was seen to shake her fist at the house, and there-
after to flatten herself in the ditch and from that position to
make an unusually offensive sign which his Worship's horse
could not pass. When urged it threw him. Any injury to
him would be a grievous blow to you all, loved as he is for
his integrity and generosity. (*Murmurs of approval in the Court.*)
You must all be shocked that anyone could wish him ill.

Sir Martin

It is yet to be proved that anyone did wish me ill. You must
prove a motive.

Upjohn

I submit that your Worship's manifest goodness would be
reason enough for the Devil's hatred.

Fiddlesticks.

UPJOHN
(*bowing*)

Your Worship is modest. With characteristic kindness Sir Martin had Alison Taylor brought into his house for a meal, which she repaid by casting the Evil Eye, or as it is commonly called "overlooking" a little dog, the pet of the household, which has since died. (*Hostile murmurs.*)

When arrested three hours later she was eight miles away—you may wonder how she got so far—(*voice* "On a broomstick") asleep in a hay-loft. A black cat was with her, which on seeing my men leapt through the window. One must not rule out the possibility of a "Familiar" nor fail to imagine what blacker deeds, what more dreadful powers, may lurk behind the simple facts of the accusation that I bring.

SIR MARTIN

The simple facts of your accusation have yet to be proved. The blacker deeds are so far entirely imaginary. You can leave them out.

UPJOHN

Your Worship. I will call my first witnesses.

CLERK

Mistress Philippa and Mistress Bess. You must take the oath. Hold the Holy Bible in your left hand. Without your gloves, please. Put your first finger on the text where the Bible is open and say after me—I swear before Almighty God

PHILIPPA

I swear before Almighty God

CLERK

To speak the truth

PHILIPPA

To speak the truth

CLERK

The whole truth

PHILIPPA

The whole truth

CLERK

And nothing but the truth

PHILIPPA

And nothing but the truth

CLERK

So help me God.

PHILIPPA

So help me God.

CLERK

Mistress Bess. (*Repeats the oath with Bess.*)

SIR MARTIN
(*stands*)

My daughters, remember your immortal souls. (*Sits.*)

UPJOHN

Mistress Philippa, you are the eldest daughter of Sir Martin?

PHILIPPA

Yes.

64

UPJOHN

And you the second?

BESS

Yes.

UPJOHN

You have been brought up in his house?

PHILIPPA AND BESS

Yes.

UPJOHN

You revere him both as your father and as the good man we all know him to be?

PHILIPPA

(*startled and frightened*)

Yes.

BESS

Yes.

UPJOHN

Then your witness can hardly be doubted, coming from the honourable daughters of an honourable man. When did you first see the accused?

PHILIPPA

Through the window. The boys were trying to drive her away.

UPJOHN

She was quite near the house and you could see her clearly?

PHILIPPA AND BESS

Yes.

UPJOHN

What first aroused your suspicions?

PHILIPPA

She shook her fist at the house.

BESS

(*cautiously*)

I didn't see that.

UPJOHN

Did you see her go into the ditch?

PHILIPPA AND BESS

Yes. Yes.

UPJOHN

Did she fall?

PHILIPPA

She didn't exactly fall. She crouched like an animal and ran; and then she rolled over.

BESS

Yes, like that.

UPJOHN

On to her back?

PHILIPPA

Yes.

UPJOHN

Where she made this blasphemous sign?

BESS
(*inaudibly*)

Yes.

CLERK

Speak up, please.

PHILIPPA
(*looking full at Upjohn*)

Yes.

UPJOHN

Mistress Bess, you were very properly shocked. Did you see your father fall?

BESS

No. We had left the window.

UPJOHN

But you both saw him come in muddy and heard his explanation.

PHILIPPA AND BESS

Yes.

UPJOHN

I also have a statement from him. What happened when Alison Taylor came into the house?

PHILIPPA

Fido barked.

UPJOHN

It is said that dogs are particularly sensitive to the supernatural. The smell of her familiar may have been about her.

The Court should remember that all dogs bark at all strangers.
Which is why we keep them.

UPJOHN

But Alison Taylor showed an unusual dislike and fear of the
dog?

PHILIPPA

She pointed at it . . .

BESS

And her face went all withered and screwed up like a monkey's,
and she glared.

UPJOHN

What happened to the dog?

BESS

. . . it died (*almost inaudible*).

UPJOHN

It died.

(*Cries of* Boo! Duck her! Hang her!)

It died. It might have been either of you. If this woman is
a witch, and if she should be wrongfully acquitted, every
witness at this trial, their Worships, myself, and every one
of you in the crowd who has cried out against her, would be
in danger. Remember that witches are seldom acting singly.
Farmers say, "Where you see one rat there are a hundred
unseen". I say, where you see one witch there are twelve
more. They are a close society, or coven, able and keen to
revenge each other. If this woman is a witch—I stress the if,
as his Worship bids me—then there must be twelve more
unsuspected witches among you now, working their dark

and horrible deeds all the more freely because you have been too easy-going, too trustful. Think then for a moment. The hare that crosses your path in the fields; the chuckle of a jackdaw on your roof; the croak of the bull-frog behind you; the silent flight of owl or bat; the fearful yell of cats in the night; the laughter under the eaves; even the rustle of mice behind the wainscot may be the outward sign of that inward, invisible, spreading terror.

FEVER

Merciful heaven!

FRANCIS

(stands with hand raised to command silence. Pause)
I have kept this moment's silence because it seemed ungenerous to end Mr. Prosecutor's satisfaction in his own rolling rhetoric so soon with the little pin of common sense. When were Englishmen afraid of frogs and mice? Admittedly a dog has been poisoned. There is no evidence to show who did it, or if it was from something the dog picked up. I shall not cross-examine my two sisters at this point, because I know too well their talent for make-believe.

UPJOHN

My learned and juvenile friend is newly come from Cambridge, always a centre of that disbelief in spiritual powers, which he calls common sense. These are the opinions of youth. I am not much older myself, but I have already outgrown them. I will call the boys, none of whom have been corrupted with modern learning.

CLERK

Robert Ball, George Carp, Mat Price, Ben Goose, Tommy

Vines. (*They take the oath all together like a school repetition.*)

SIR MARTIN

Do you understand what you have sworn?

BOYS

Yes, your Worship.

SIR MARTIN

Do you believe in God?

BOYS

Yes, your Worship.

SIR MARTIN

Then mind what you say.

UPJOHN

Now, boys, your parents are all tenants of Sir Martin?

BOYS

Yes, Sir.

UPJOHN

You all know him and respect him?

BOYS

Yes, Sir.

UPJOHN

You would not willingly let anyone harm him?

BOYS

No, Sir.

UPJOHN

You did in fact try to drive Alison Taylor away from his gate? (*Surprise.*)

70

ROBERT

Yes, Sir. (*The others all look at him.*)

UPJOHN

You were the leader in coming to his Worship's defence?

ROBERT

Yes, Sir.

SIR MARTIN

Mr. Prosecutor, I cannot allow it to be thought that pelting an old woman with mud and stones can ever earn my gratitude. Boys will pelt anything. It could as easily have been my windows, and often is.

UPJOHN

Your Worship. Where did you first see the wi . . . this woman?

ROBERT

About half a mile back.

UPJOHN

What made you suspect her?

GEORGE

She was a foreigner.

MAT

Foreigners is up to no good.

GEORGE

We don't want them.

UPJOHN

What was she doing?

MAT

Talking to herself.

BEN GOOSE

An' talking to a cat on the wall.

UPJOHN

Was she, indeed? Did she *fondle* it particularly? Could you hear what she said to it?

BEN

A' scratched it under the chin and mumbled a lot of silly stuff.

UPJOHN

It might not have seemed so silly if you had understood it. Did the cat seem to know her?

BEN

It arched its back and held its tail up like they do. (*Draws it in the air tail last, as if stroking it.*)

UPJOHN

Did it seem to be hers?

TOMMY

Please, Sir, it was my auntie's cat. (*Laughter.*)

UPJOHN

Be careful, little boy, how you bring your auntie into this. Two witches often share a familiar devil, which may be in the form of a cat.

TOMMY

My auntie's not a witch, and she hasn't got a devil. (*Laughter.*)

UPJOHN

This little witness is not yet very wise about women. Not many married men would agree with him. (*Laughter.*) Have you ever seen the Devil, Tommy?

TOMMY

No, Sir.

UPJOHN

Then how would you recognize him if you saw him? Now, boys. Was the old woman making straight for Sir Martin's house?

ROBERT

Yes, Sir.

UPJOHN

And you couldn't get her to change her direction?

ROBERT

No, Sir.

UPJOHN

Did she hiss or spit at you?

BEN

She mewed like a cat when a mud ball hit her in the mouth. (*Boys titter.*)

UPJOHN

Come now, this is a serious matter. When she was by the house, did she show any hostility?

ROBERT, GEORGE, MAT AND BEN
(*in chorus as if taught*)

She shook her fist at it.

73

TOMMY

But that was because . . .

UPJOHN

That's enough, Tommy. My question has been answered.

SIR MARTIN

Mr. Prosecutor, I think we should hear what this very spontaneous witness has to say. Go on, Tommy. That was because?

TOMMY

Because the young lady was throwing at her too, out of the window.

Boys nudge him and whisper "Justice's daughter you daft little . . ."

SIR MARTIN

Which young lady, Tommy? Don't be afraid.

(*Tommy points silently at Bess. Murmurs in the crowd.*)

SIR MARTIN

(*wearily*)

Question her, Mr. Prosecutor.

UPJOHN

I would like to submit that the last witness is too young to be of any reliability in court.

Mistress Bess, what do you say to this unlikely suggestion from our little witness? For my part your grace and good breeding make it quite impossible to believe.

BESS

I was eating an apple and it had a maggot in it, so I opened the lattice and threw it out.

PHILIPPA

That's right. And the old woman had shaken her fist before the apple was thrown away.

UPJOHN

I think I have made my point.

FRANCIS

I shall not take much of the Court's time in dismissing my learned friend's fairy story about a heroic band of boys confronting the Devil. It was quite a feat to make so much out of so little. What? A lonely old woman stops to stroke a cat? Which of us can resist a cat that asks to be stroked, as Ben Goose so neatly showed us? You will hardly condemn anyone to death for that. As for the ominous shaken fist, would it not have been natural to shake it at any one of those plaguing boys? For that is all they were. Just idle young bullies.

VOICE

Don't you call our Robert a bully.

VOICE

What about your sister?

UPJOHN

Call my next witness.

Mistress Jenny.

(*Jenny takes the oath quietly and without prompting.*)

UPJOHN

Did you see the prisoner, Alison Taylor, in your father's ante-room?

JENNY

Yes, Sir.

UPJOHN

Did your dog Fido bark at her?

JENNY

Yes, Sir, just a woof.

UPJOHN

He was not a very good watch dog?

JENNY

Yes, Sir, he was.

UPJOHN

Why, if it was only one Woof! as you say, was she so vexed?

JENNY

There were dogs with the boys outside, and they had been fierce. I heard them.

UPJOHN

So she was vexed?

JENNY

I think she was frightened.

UPJOHN

Did she then point her finger at Fido?

JENNY

Yes. And I picked him up.

UPJOHN

Nevertheless, she cast the Evil Eye on him?

JENNY

She didn't look any different from anyone else.

UPJOHN

But all the same, Fido died?
(*Jenny weeps.*)
He died, didn't he?
(*She nods.*)
(*Rhythmic shouts of* "Witch, Witch, Witch, Witch".)

UPJOHN

Thank you. I need not ask you any more.

FRANCIS

Jenny, you are very sad about Fido; but do you really
believe it was the Evil Eye that killed him?

JENNY

No. My sisters are always making up stories. I can't believe
the real Devil was peeping out from under the old woman's
skirts.
(*Murmurs of excitement and belief, in which Fever joins.*)
Or that he jumped up the chimney. Nobody over three
could believe that.

77

FRANCIS

Is that what your sisters said?

JENNY

Yes. Bess said she jerked the old woman's stool away to make the Devil run out, and Philippa said she saw him leap up the chimney. Who would believe that?

FRANCIS

Some grown-up people would.

JENNY

They must be very silly people.

FRANCIS

So you don't believe any of it?

JENNY

No.

FRANCIS

Thank you, Jenny. That's all.

UPJOHN

Mistress Philippa. Your sister Jenny has cast doubts upon the evidence that you gave under oath. I think you should be given the chance of clearing away any suspicion of perjury that might arise. Though your sister Jenny is very young to give evidence in court, yet suspicion sticks. I should be sorry to see so beautiful and promising a young lady as yourself dishonoured, and her whole future blighted for want of instant confirmation of the evidence. Let us look for it.

Do you agree that Mistress Bess, suspecting the Devil, pulled away the stool from under the prisoner?

PHILIPPA

Yes, Sir, she did.

UPJOHN

And did the prisoner fall?

PHILIPPA

Yes, she did. And spilt all her soup.

UPJOHN

Did she not hurt herself?

PHILIPPA

She hurt her elbow.

UPJOHN

But you yourself did the prisoner no personal injury?

PHILIPPA

No.

UPJOHN

Is it not odd that after such an affront from your sister Bess, the prisoner should have cast the Evil Eye on Fido, who is dead, and not rather on your sister? Was she not the obvious victim?

PHILIPPA

Oh. She cast it on Bess too.
(*Dead silence in the Court.*)

BESS

You couldn't! You wouldn't da——

UPJOHN

She cast it on Bess too.

(*Bess falls in a dead faint.*)

We cannot doubt that she did.

(*Uproar in the Court. Cries of* "Duck the Witch, Duck the Witch, Duck the Witch". *The Physician comes to Bess and he and Alice carry her out, followed by Jenny.*)

GIRTH, FEVER AND DE GROOT

(*after conferring, to Sir Martin*)

Let the prisoner be taken and ducked.

DE GROOT

Let her be ducked first and hanged afterwards.

SIR MARTIN

I cannot agree with you, gentlemen. That the guilty float and the innocent sink, is a theory impossible of proof. But you overrule me. Constables, let Alison Taylor be taken and ducked, but see that she has fair treatment. Afterwards let her be taken back to her cell. The trial is adjourned till to-morrow. Go with them, Parson, and use your influence. Francis, go and do what you can. See that the rope is good, and if they don't drown her, give her this cordial. Mr. Mayor?

(*The Mayor shrugs. Constables lead out Alison Taylor. The Justices go out, the court clears in wild excitement. Mr. Upjohn offers his arm to Philippa.*)

UPJOHN

Shall we go and watch?

A FURTIVE MAN

Sir, you'll find a name writ here that might interest you, but I'd be glad if mine need not come into it.

UPJOHN

I'll look into it. (*Tips him.*)
Come, my young beauty. Let's see the sport.

CURTAIN

SCENE II

The ante-room.
Bess lying on a bench in front of fire. Alice, Jenny and Physician slapping Bess's hand.

PHYSICIAN

It is a very deep faint.

ALICE

It is just the excitement of the Court. At her age it is quite usual. (*Slaps her face.*)
Bess! Bess!!

PHYSICIAN

Her pulse is low. Burnt feathers might bring her round.

ALICE

Run, Jenny, to the kitchen. There are pheasants there.
(*Exit Jenny.*)

PHYSICIAN

It was a very strange attack, happening like that. It has doomed that old creature.

(*Re-enter Jenny with feathers.*)

Her pulse flutters. There, that's better. She's coming round. Dame Alice, some hot milk and brandy, if you can.

BESS

Oh, Jenny! Stay with me, Jenny. Don't let them do it. I know they mean to.

JENNY

Do what, Bess? You are still dreaming.

BESS

I'm frightened. Stay, Jenny. Never leave me alone.
(*Re-enter Alice.*)

ALICE

Drink this, Bess. You'll feel better.

BESS

What is it? Milk! No, No. I won't.

ALICE

Come along. The physician says you are to have it. (*Tries to make her drink.*)

BESS

No no no no (*fights*).

PHYSICIAN

We won't force her, lest she faint again. Let her rest, and her sister stay by her.

(*Bess weeps with her face in the pillow.*)

She'll do now.
(*Wild shouts outside.*)
I may be wanted after the ducking. Shall we go? You
wouldn't want to miss it.

ALICE

No, indeed.
(*Exeunt Physician and Alice, right.*)

JENNY

What is it, Bess?

BESS

I'm so frightened. Oh, Jenny, I'm sorry about Fido. I really
am. I don't want to see Philippa.

JENNY

She's gone to the ducking.
(*Second round of shouting, then dead silence. Jenny rises as if to go
to the window.*)

BESS

(*clutching*)

Stay with me, Jenny. I'm frightened of Philippa. And Alice.
And Mr. Upjohn. They are all bad. I want Father. I'm not
frightened of him. I know he's terribly angry with me, but
he would never do anything bad. I know he wouldn't.
(*Wild shouting, continuous and approaching.*)

BESS

Don't go.
(*Enter Sir Martin, sternly.*)

SIR MARTIN

Well, Bess. Was this play-acting?

BESS

(into pillow)

No, Father.

JENNY

It was a bad faint, Father. She was so long coming round, I couldn't help wondering if she was . . . like Fido.
(Bess sobs.)

SIR MARTIN

You have done a bad day's work, and if this faint was feigned, it was the Devil's own idea.

BESS

It wasn't pretence, really it wasn't. It had got too horrible. Father! I need you. I don't mind what you do to me.

SIR MARTIN

If this is repentance, it is good, though it comes too late. Real or pretence, your faint has doomed poor old Alison.

JENNY

There was such a dreadful shouting, Father. What has happened?

SIR MARTIN

I was glad you were not there, my love, to see such barbarity. They stripped her and tied her hands and feet and threw her in, and she sank. Then she came up again three times, as they say all drowning persons do, and Francis pulled her out. Then Fever and De Groot said "Throw her in again". They did, poor old thing. She was blue and shivering—it was bitterly cold. This time she only came up twice but was pulled out coughing.

84

JENNY

And then?

SIR MARTIN

And then that scoundrel Upjohn inflamed the crowd so that they clamoured for a third trial. And Francis said, in that case he would be thrown in too, in the same way, so that they could compare his sinking with hers. The two constables tied him and threw him in, and Walter and the kennelman held the ropes. You must have heard the shouting then. The old woman had no breath left in her old body at all, and she sank like a stone, but Francis's back floated like a raft though his face was under water. However, the kennelman looked after him, and he's all right.

JENNY

And old Alison?

SIR MARTIN

Walter pulled her out. The Parson and the Physician did what they could to get the water out of her, and Francis shared his brandy with her. That dreadful Witch Searcher dressed her and they took her away to her cell. There'll be no fire there to warm her.

JENNY

Couldn't we send her one?

SIR MARTIN

My darling child! Yes, we could.
Walter! Walter!
(*Enter Walter.*)

WALTER

Yes, Sir?

SIR MARTIN

Tell the blacksmith to get the brazier out of the armoury and take it down to the lock-up, with a good barrow of small logs, to make a fire for the prisoner. Here's a shilling for the Turnkey. Tell him I sent you. And do you get a basket of food from Cook and take that to her. She is not yet proved guilty.

WALTER

I'll be glad to do it, Sir. The old woman was more dead than alive. She takes it all as patient and helpless as an ill-used dog. I don't like to see it.

SIR MARTIN

You're a good boy, Walter. You did all you could for her.

(*Exit Walter. Enter Philippa pink-cheeked and laughing, followed by Alice.*)

PHILIPPA

What an afternoon! I haven't laughed so much for ages. Pity you weren't there, Bess. I couldn't have laughed more, unless they'd thrown in Father and the Bishop instead of Francis.

(*Sees her father and scoots upstairs. Exit via gallery left.*)

SIR MARTIN

Wretched girl. Does innocence and injustice mean nothing to you? Mistress Alice, have you no influence on her?

ALICE

I do my best, Sir, but girls of that age will not be told anything. How should she listen to me if she will not listen to you?

Sir Martin

Because you are young, and a woman.

(*Enter Francis.*)

Well done, my son. Come to the fire. I am sure you need it.

Francis

I am warmer now, thank you, Sir. The water felt as cold as a sword. (*To Bess*) Well, sister, your ill-timed faint turned everyone against us. Why did you have to faint just at that moment? I have to thank you for my ducking. Forgive me for getting between you and the fire. You'd better be cured by Monday.

Alice

I will see that she has plenty of good food and cordials. I shall make it my business.

Bess

No. No. I don't want anything. I won't eat anything.

Sir Martin

You will do as you are told.

Bess

I can't, Father.

Sir Martin

She should be in bed in her room. Take her up, Mistress Alice.

Bess

Not with Philippa. Please, please, Father, not with Philippa. Please, Father, let me be in Jenny's room.

ALICE

Girls! Girls! One whim after another. Come with me, Bess.

SIR MARTIN

I should not wish to be with Philippa myself, after her exhibition today. Jenny, will you have Bess with you?

JENNY

Yes. I'll look after her.

BESS

Thank you, Jenny.

(*Enter Upjohn.*)

Don't leave me.

UPJOHN

Well, Master Francis. I have never had that trick played on me by Defence before. You are full of ingenuity. It was a blow to our three Justices. They will talk of nothing else till Monday, and probably for a year after. There's nothing like making a real show of it. The whole neighbourhood will be buzzing. They don't often have the chance to see the Squire's son sail through the air and go in splosh. Incidentally, you wet me through. This story will get to London and make laughing stocks of us both. And how is our little invalid? You have won our case for us.

(*Bess starts away but fails to get on her feet.*)

JENNY

Help me please, Francis. We'll take her up to my room.
(*Francis carries her up. Exeunt.*)

SIR MARTIN

Excuse me, Mr. Upjohn, if I go to my room till supper. I

am very tired and I think we have little to say to each other.
You have a good fire. Tobacco here if you have a pipe.
Mistress Alice will bring you wine.
(*Exit, centre back.*)

UPJOHN

We will drink to our success so far, Alice. I have been given
three more names today. Here. Look at these. Are any of
them our people?

ALICE

These? No! Contemptible envy and childish revenges.
Nothings.

UPJOHN

Seeds then of large harvests. Look at our good Justice Martin
and his daughters. May his heart break! (*Pours a second glass.*)
To old Chaos.

ALICE

(*drinks to him*)

My lord!

UPJOHN

It will be Candlemas on Monday. Where do you meet?

ALICE

On Herne Fen.

UPJOHN

The Grand Master will be attending. (*Deep reverence from
Alice.*)
At what time can you leave?

ALICE

A little before midnight. But I must be back by cockcrow.

UPJOHN

You ride behind me on the Black Horse. On Herne Fen we
will dance together the Dance of the Horned Beasts.

CURTAIN

SCENE III

The Court Room. Two days later.
The second day of the trial is in progress. The Justices are sitting.
Witnesses, notables, crowds, constables as before. Alison Taylor
mumbles continuously as if in delirium. Alice, Cook and kennelman
are the only witnesses. Philippa with notables.

SIR MARTIN

Let the prisoner be seated. It is clear she can hardly stand.
(*Constable brings her a stool.*)

ALISON TAYLOR

Let me sit by the fire. There's nothing like a good fire.

UPJOHN

Your Worships, it must be admitted, however reluctantly,
that the ordeal by water gave no clear proof of the prisoner's
guilt. And though Sir Martin's kennelman was of the opinion
that the dog died by poison, it must be remembered that
witches are skilled in poison and can kill at a distance by
sending a familiar flea to inject it into the victim's veins.
(*Fever huddles up into his cloak and signs to the court to stand
back from the prisoner.*)
The witness of Sir Martin's cook confirms that Mistress Bess
both insulted and injured the prisoner. We must therefore

give great weight to Mistress Alice's account of that young lady.

Mistress Alice, how is his Worship's daughter Bess since her seizure in the Court here on Saturday?

ALICE

She is very ill. She has had no food or drink these three days. She cannot swallow and spits out all we give her.

UPJOHN

What reason does she give for refusing food and drink?

ALICE

She will not speak nor answer, either to me or to her eldest sister Philippa, though till now they were never apart.

UPJOHN

Is her mind affected?

ALICE

She has fits of unreason and screams if approached.

UPJOHN

How does she receive her father?

ALICE

She covers her face with the bedclothes.

UPJOHN

Your Worships, this is surely as clear a case of the Evil Eye as you are ever likely to hear of. It is as if the Devil, resenting her father's manifest disbelief, should strike down a daughter of the house to prove his power.

Francis

It is at least as likely that my sister Bess, who is only twelve years old, should be violently repenting her silly stories on seeing where they lead. Look, your Worships, and all of you in the court room at that poor old woman there.

(*Alison Taylor has stopped muttering and wheezing and sits huddled and bent, her head nearly on her knees.*)

She should rather have been given a pension and found a room in an almshouse than be treated with the inhumanity we have all seen. I implore you, find more mercy in your hearts than fear.

Sir Martin

Gentlemen, we have heard all the evidence and must now agree on our decision. I am bitterly ashamed of my two daughters, and for my part do not believe a word that they have said.

Fever

But the dog was bewitched, and your daughter, too. You can't overlook that. Do you not care for your own daughter? Then how can you care for the rest of us? My blood runs cold.

Girth

She has done two bewitchments, that's a fact. They can't both be coincidence.

de Groot

There's no two ways about it. She is guilty without any doubt, of the worst crime there is. She should suffer the worst punishment. She should be hanged.

Sir Martin

It is not in the power of this Court to pass sentence. You

are three to one. Do you wish her to be kept in prison until the Assizes and re-tried then?

GIRTH, FEVER AND DE GROOT

We do.

SIR MARTIN

I wish to dissociate myself from my three colleagues who find the evidence against the prisoner sufficient.
Alison Taylor, you have been presumed guilty of witchcraft and are to be confined in prison until the Assizes.
(*Uproar in Court and a minute later cheering outside.*)
Constable, take the prisoner back to her cell.
(*The constable shakes Alison Taylor by the shoulder and she falls to the floor.*)

CONSTABLE

Your Worships—she's dead.

DE GROOT

Why, damnation, she can't be hanged if she's dead!
(*Physician comes forward—confusion. Outside the cheering has changed to a sound like the buzzing of bees.*)

CURTAIN

SCENE IV

The ante-room.
Walter in attendance. Enter right Sir Martin, Francis, Parson, Physician.

SIR MARTIN

It is good of you, my old friends, to come in with me

tonight. I need your company. Why could they not have shown her some sympathy before she died? You would think now that she was everybody's grandmother.

FRANCIS

These are people I have grown up among, and they enjoyed the ducking like a day's sport. I shall never feel the same to them again.

(*Enter Jenny from upstairs with a mug. Curtsies to all as she goes.*)

SIR MARTIN

Here is one who will always be the same. Where are you off to, my love?

JENNY

I am getting some milk for Bess. She will take what I give her, if I get it myself.

(*Exit to kitchen and then upstairs.*)

FRANCIS

I suspect Philippa and Bess of more guilt than we know.

SIR MARTIN

Don't speak to me of them. I fear I must find another house-keeper. For all her breeding, she fails to have the right influence. Come, my friends—in here.

(*Exeunt centre back.*)

(*Enter right Alice and Philippa. Upjohn's back can be partly seen in entrance right. Alice goes through into the kitchen left. Philippa hangs about waiting for Upjohn. He enters but does not acknowledge her bob curtsy. She runs forward.*)

PHILIPPA

Wasn't it splendid? You won your case. I knew you would, of course. And I did help, didn't I?

UPJOHN

Did I ask you your help?

PHILIPPA

No, of course you didn't. But I gave it, didn't I! You could say thank you.

UPJOHN
(*bowing*)

Too kind.

PHILIPPA

Isn't that what you wanted? Aren't you pleased?

UPJOHN

Pleased! You brainless girl, can't you see that now she's dead all the sympathy is turned the other way? Nobody will be found now to incriminate their neighbours—until they've forgotten the old hag. It's her ghost they'll fear now. And so should you. If only she had lived long enough to be hanged.

PHILIPPA

But it wasn't my fault that she died. You are unfair.

UPJOHN

Unfair! Unfair! Do you think I bother about being fair, you nonentity? Were you fair to the old creature? Hang them all! I want spectacular results.

PHILIPPA

Oh.

UPJOHN

I'll be as unfair as the law allows, but it will be a waste of time here for—weeks. I don't waste weeks. I shall be moving on tonight.

PHILIPPA

Tonight? You're not going? For always?

UPJOHN

With your permission.

PHILIPPA

Take me with you. You can't leave me with Father. I don't know what he will do to me. Let me come with you. Take me. It was all only for you.

UPJOHN

You are tiresome. Tell your father, with my most reverent compliments of course, that I am dining with Justice de Groot this evening before leaving. My servants will come for my baggage. Adieu, Mistress Philippa.

(*Exit right. Philippa runs upstairs and throws herself weeping on her bed.*)

CURTAIN

SCENE V

The ante-room, later that night.

Moonlight through window right. The house in darkness. Enter

96

above, Alice carrying a candle. She is wearing a mask and a hood. She comes down slowly, sets the door right ajar, puts out the candle. Presently the door is pushed open and bright moonlight throws on screen the shadow of Upjohn in bull's mask. Enter Upjohn.)

UPJOHN

The fire is lit. It is time. Come, they are waiting for us.

ALICE

I have a good account to give them. I have tonight done what must be done to raise a ghost.

UPJOHN

You are never idle.

ALICE

It was not difficult, being but a poor spirit and hardly yet detached. I charged it with the power and malice that it lacked.

UPJOHN

Well done. You have a pleasant genius for evil.

ALICE

The Horned Man is my god.

(*Exeunt.*)

CURTAIN

SCENE VI

The girls' bedroom.

Sounds of horse galloping into distance. Silence. Upstairs alone in her room, Philippa, weeping, lights her candle.

97

I can't bear it. I'm so miserable. I wish Bess was here. God!
I might have poisoned her if he had needed it. How could
he be so cruel? What shall I do? Father will send me away.
Nobody loves me. *He* doesn't. Oh, oh I can't believe it. I
must talk to somebody. I shall go mad.

(*Gets up and knocks on door.*)

Alice! Alice! (*Opens door.*) Alice!
She's not there! I am all alone. Where can she be? The night
seems to have stopped moving, it will never end. It's as if
somebody had made a hole in time. Brr! I've got the shud-
ders. Perhaps I can see the time on the church clock by moonlight.

(*From her bed pulls the curtain and opens the window.*)

There's a fire somewhere over there. The clouds are red
underneath. There's something going on somewhere. I can
feel it. But not here. It's the Nothingness that's going on
here that frightens me. Aah! I'm young and I'm pretty and
I'm alive, and he has left me. It's all because of that old dead
hag. What did she matter anyway? She was old.

(*Twelve o'clock strikes.*)

What's that rustling in the ivy?

(*Pushing through the lattice comes the fumbling black bundle of the
old woman's ghost.*)

Philippa tries to scream but almost no sound comes.

CURTAIN